PLAYING
SOCCER

SEAN FINNIGAN

Soccer is a fun sport.

Here is a soccer ball.

Here is a soccer goal.

Look at the girl.

The girl is kicking the ball.

Look at the boy.

The boy is kicking the ball.

The soccer ball
is going up, up, up!

The soccer ball
is in the goal!

GLOSSARY

soccer ball

goal

kick